Power against Unclean SPIRITS

Dr. D. K. Olukoya

POWER AGAINST UNCLEAN SPIRITS
© 2011 DR. D. K. OLUKOYA
ISBN **978-0692543344**
January 2011

Publ ished by:
Mountain of Fire and Miracles Ministries Press
13, Olasimbo Street, Onike, Yaba, Lagos.

*I salute my wonderful wife, Pastor Shade, for her
invaluable support in the ministry.*
*I appreciate her unquantifiable support in the book ministry
as the cover designer, art ed itor and art advisor*

All Scripture quotation is from the King James Version of
the Bible

Dr. D.K Olukoya

CONTENTS

4

Power Against Unclean Spirits

Dr. D.K Olukoya

CHAPTER ONE

POWER

Against

UNCLEAN

SPIRITS

The world we live in is filled with foul spirits. These unclean spirits have polluted the lives of many all over the world. The principal assignment of an unclean spirit is to carry out evil assignments. If you want to enjoy your life and fulfill your destiny, you must paralyse them and put an end to their evil activities and plans.

The Bible lets us know that God has given believers the authority to be able to do certain things. We have to learn about those things and walk in that authority which is the birthright of every child of God.

One area of authority is the ability to overcome sin, and all the bad habits in every area of our lives:

> *"And she shall bring forth a Son, and thou shalt call his name JESUS: for he shall save his people from their sins."* **Matthew 1: 21.**

The Bible also says, "In whom we have forgiveness, we have redemption." Therefore, we have been given power from God to overcome sin and evil habits. As from today, you have to walk in this authority that God has given you.

SPIRITUAL IMMUNITY
Another area in which we have been given authority is in our immunity against poison, and the control of wild beasts:

> *"Behold I give unto you power to tread on serpents and scorpions, and over all the power of the enemy; and nothing shall by any means hurt you."*
> **Luke 10:19.**

In add iton to these, we have also been given the authority to heal the sick:

> *"Is any sick among you? let him call for the elders of the church; and let them pray over him, anointing him with oil in the name of the Lord."*
> **James 5: 14.**

Similarly, **Mark 16:17** says: *"And these signs shall follow them that believe. In my name shall they cast out demons; they shall speak with new tongues. They shall lay hands on the sick, and the sick shall recover."*

control the elements and perform all kinds of miracles in His name. This explains why Joshua was able to command the sun to stand still and work in his favour **(Joshua 10:12).**

Another thing that the Bible gives us authority to do is, to execute judgment upon the powers of darkness:

> *"Let the high praises of God be in their mouth, and a two-edged sword in their hand.*

Furthermore, it should interest you to know that you and I have also been given authority to raise the dead:

> *"Verily, verily, I say unto you, He that believeth on me, the works that I do shall he do also, and greater works than these shall he do, because I go unto my Father."* **John 14: 12.**

Jesus raised the dead and, by this decree, He has given us the authority to be able to raise the dead just as He did.

Another authority that the Lord Jesus Christ promises us is the authority to bind and loose:-

> *"Verily, I say unto you, whatsoever ye shall bind on earth shall be bound in heaven and whatsoever ye shall loose on earth shall be loosed in heaven."* **Matthew 18: 18.**

Dr. D.K Olukoya

To execute vengeance upon the heathen, and punishments upon the people." **Psalm 149:67.**

So, we are authorised to execute judgment, not on one another or on Pastors and Ministers of God, but on all the works of darkness. You are to judge yourself, and also the powers of darkness.

AUTHORITY TO DESTROY

The authority to destroy he works of satan is another authority that the Word of God promises us as believers. Also, Jesus Christ has given us authority to be able to

The Bible promises us is the authority to obtain abundant provision for living:

> *"But my God shall supply all your need according to his riches in glory by Christ Jesus."* **Philippians 4:19.**

There is more. The Word of God also promises us the authority to have complete knowledge of the truth in the Word of God, beyond all doubt. That is why the Bible says:

> *"Study to show thyself approved unto God, a workman that needeth not to be ashamed, rightly dividing the word of truth."* **2 Timothy 2:15.**

We, as believers, have also been given the authority to experience the rivers of living water flowing out of our innermost being.

> *"In the last day, that great day of the feast, Jesus stood and cried, saying, If any man thirst, let him come unto me, and drink. He that believeth on me, as the scripture hath said, out of his belly shall flow rivers of living water. (But this spake he of the Spirit which they that believe on him should receive: for the Holy Ghost was not given; because that Jesus was not yet glorified)."* **John 7: 37-39.**

RIVERS OF LIVING WATER

As we read in the last passage, we have the authority to have rivers of living water flowing out of our innermost being. We also have the authority to do the work of Christ; including the authority to do greater works than He did. Believers, we have authority to have freedom from darkness and experience fullness in all areas of our lives. Additionally, we have authority over sound health, and to remain in sound health.

Moreover, we have the authority to receive the fruit of the Spirit, and impart it to others.

Finally, we have been given the authority to exercise power over all unclean spirits.

> "And when he had called unto him his twelve disciples, he gave them power against unclean spirits, to cast them out, and to heal all manner of sickness and all manner of disease." **Matthew 10:1.**

Let us look at another passage from the Word of God that also confirms this :

> "And he called unto him the twelve, and began to send them forth by two and two, and gave them power over unclean spirits." **Mark 6:7.**

> "After these things the Lord appointed other seventy also, and sent them two by two before his face, into every city and place, whither he himself would come." **Luke 10:1.**

We can see from these Scriptures that, as the disciples were sent out, they were given power to be able to stand against unclean spirits. When they came back, their report was that they saw satan himself falling before them.

The Holy Spirit is the Spirit of God. Likewise unclean spirits are the spirits that come from the devil. They are obedient and are in subjection to him. We need not argue about whether or not there are demons, or whether unclean spirits exist or not. Whether you believe it or not, the Word of God has said that there are unclean spirits; Jesus also made us to know that there are unclean spirits. Also, whether or not you doubt the existence of satan, the fact remains that satan exists as well. What is more important however, is knowlegdge of what we can do against these unclean spirits.

UNCLEANS SPIRITS

Unclean spirits are rampant in our society today and can be encountered in different places. They are personalities, i.e. spirit beings that exist spiritually, although they often appear physically as well. We need not know how they came to the earth, but the Bible says they came to the surface of the earth. Although they don't have physical bodies, one of their aims is to possess human beings so they can carry out their activities on the surface of the earth.

Unclean spirits express their will and personality in our natural world, by attaching themselves to objects, especially those which have been dedicated to them. They attach themselves to idols, amulets, charms, fetish materials and instruments of ritual worship. Anyone who has any charm, concoction, amulet or idol at home has a ready material for unclean spirits. Such a person would be attacked or oppressed day and night.

Apart from using or looking for human beings to possess, they can also inhabit physical places such as houses, buildings or an apartment within a building.

There are other names that the Bible uses when referring to unclean spirits. One of them is seducing spirits.

> *"Now the Spirit speaketh expressly that in the latter times, some shall depart from the faith, giving heed to seducing spirits, and doctrines of devils."*
> **1 Timothy 4:1.**

> *"Then goeth he, and taketh with himself seven other spirits more wicked than himself, and they enter in and dwell there, and the last state of that man is worse than the first. Even so shall it be also unto this wicked generation."*
> **Matthew 12: 45.**

The Bible makes it very clear that there are evil spirits, and it is our responsibility to war against them.

At this juncture, please take this prayer point: "My life is not the habitation of evil spirits. My body is the temple of the living God therefore, no power of darkness can enter into me, in the name of Jesus."

The Word of God also calls them devil's agents; and in addition, it calls them principalities and powers.

"For we wrestle not against flesh and blood, but against principalities, against powers, against the rulers of darkness of this world, against spiritual wickedness in high places." **Ephesians 6:12.**

Beloved, whatever the name they are called, they are unclean spirits. They are not holy and that therefore qualifies them to be called unclean spirits.

FEATURES OF UNCLEAN SPIRITS

1. **They can speak.**
    When Jesus went to the temple, the first personalities to recognise Him were demons. The Pharisees, the Saducees, the High Priests, and the Teachers that were there did not realise who He was. However, immediately the person that was possessed with demons saw Him, he said, "What have you to do with us, Jesus of Nazareth? Have you come to torment us before our time?"

2. **They have understanding and they are very intelligent.**
    The Bible says that the children of darkness are wiser in their generation than the children of light. Any Christian that chooses to copy the ways of unbelievers is undoing

himself. If those being copied are children of darkness, he will be unable to recognise that they are demonic spirits and, because they are wiser in their own generation, they would easily ruin him. Unbelievers can commit sin and get away with it because it is part of their life. If a believer copies them, one day he or she will be caught.

3. **They can believe to a limited extent.**

The Bible says that there is only one God. The demons also believe that. They also believe that Jesus exists too; however, they don't want to accept that Jesus is greater than them.

4. **They co-operate with one another.**

Sometimes, the one that has greater demons would cast out the one with lesser demons, and would say he is powerful. That is why sometimes you see a child of the devil say, "I am the husband of witches, I am the wife of wizards." Such a person must be using the power of the devil against the devil. So, when you go to them with a problem, they pretend to solve it but actually they replace it with another problem. They will deceive you so that you will not know that that problem is still there and is multiplying in your life. That is why we have fake prophets or white garment herbalists. They use the power of the devil to subdue smaller demons and to exercise authority over them.

5. **They seek bodies to enter and to control.**

6. **They know their end.**
They know where they are going to end up, that was why the demons in the possessed man who challenged Jesus asked Him whether He had come to torment them before their time. (Matt 8:29)

7. **They recognise divine powers.**
They know those that have divine authority. They know what you truly are spiritually. They know your spiritual level. That is why they would deal seriously with someone who is not living a clean life and wants to cast them out. The sons of Sceva wanted to cast them out, whereas they did not have the authority to do so and disaster befell them.

8. **They recognise those who have received Holy Ghost Baptism.**

    They know those that say, "Me? My own blood is bitter, nobody can suck my blood," but do not really have any power. Such people are easy prey for them. So, if you have not received the Holy Spirit, try to do so because they know who we really are spiritually. They know those that are not living a clean life and are merely saying, "Let me follow them to church, maybe one day, God will do it."

9. **They recognise those who have divine authority and can exercise it over them.** I pray that you can exercise the authority that Jesus Christ has given to you, in Jesus' name, Amen.

    THE WORKS OF UNCLEAN SPIRITS

1. **They cause spiritual blindness.**

    They do this so that whenever you are talking to their victims or preaching the gospel to them, they will not believe or agree with you. During evangelism, you will come across some people talking and arguing with you. Recognise that they are under the control of these evil sprits. What you should do in such cases is to bind the demons and you will recognise a break immediately. Spiritual blindness not only stops unbelievers from receiving the word of God, it also blinds their eyes to their sins and the consequences.

2.   **They attack the doctrines and Body of Jesus Christ.**

For example, they disagree that the death of Jesus was a substitute. Unclean spirits cause sinners to believe that God is a good God and cannot punish anybody. They also fill their hearts with hatred against ministers of the living God, and attack them wherever they preach.

3.   **They cause sicknesses.**
They possess a person in order to kill him, so that he will not be able to hear about Christ.

WHAT THEY DO TO BELIEVERS
The main objeective of unclean spirits is to deceive believers into believing that committing a sin just once is not a big deal and that God will pardon them. Immediately the believer has committed the sin, the unclean spirits will spring into action and begin to attack their lives in one way or another.   After the sin has been committed they then

report it to God and try to use it as a legal right to affl ict the bel iever. They do this by going to God and saying something l ike this: "Your son or daughter just cursed somebody on the way to fellowship. And because of that, his/her prayer should not be answered."

Unclean spirits are also responsible for the attacks on the Word of God in the l ife of many bel ievers. They make sure they render to naught the teachings of Christ in the l ife of many of His d isciples. In the Parable of the Sowers, we read about how they d istort the words of God that are planted in the hearts of people.

Sometimes they oppress bel ievers who allow themselves to be oppressed.

We are fight ing a battle against a very wise and crafty enemy. It is our duty to be wiser than the devil we f ight so we do not fall vict im to his attacks. The evil ones are wiser in their own generation, but the Bible says that you can receive the wisdom of God so that you can know how to deal with them.

WHAT DO WE DO TO THEM?

"And have no fellowship with the unfruitful works of darkness, but rather reprove them. For it is a shame even to speak of those things which are done of them in secret." **Ephesians 5: 11-12.**

The Word of God does not say we should pet evil spirits. It says, we should rebuke them. **Mark 16:17** says, *"And these signs shall follow them that believe: In my name shall they cast out demons, they shall speak with new tongues."*

The devil is a liar and has failed woefully. The Bible says, *"You shall cast out devils."* And we saw this being done in the ministry of Jesus Christ. He was always casting out devils, healing the sick and raising the dead. Paul also cast out devils. We, as believers, have been given the authority to cast out devils, and we should begin to exercise this authority n our lives.

Power of the Christian over and against unclean spirits lies in the name of Jesus.

> *"Wherefore, God also hath highly exalted him, and given him a name which is above every name. That at the name of Jesus, every knee should bow of things in heaven and things in earth, and things under the earth."* **Philippians 2: 9-10.**

We have the name of Jesus as a weapon with which we can exercise authority not only against them, but over them too. Let us take a look at **Luke 10:17:**

> *"And the seventy returned again with joy, saying,*
> *Lord, even the demons are subject unto us*
> *through thy name."*

Why were they subject to them? It is because of the name of Jesus. The name of Jesus is powerful, and very great. There is no power of the enemy, or any demon that can withstand it.

ABSOLUTE OBEDIENCE

When Jesus sent His disciples forth, He gave them power against unclean spirits to enable them cast out devils. Remember, those that were sent out were those that were called disciples or believers. They were walking in full obedience to Jesus Christ.

For you to be able to exercise power against unclean spirits, you also need to walk in full obedience to the Lord and not in partial obedience. You should not be like those who say: "My own Christianity is different. Let me be doing it little by little. Later on, I will join them." If you are like that, the unclean spirits will attack you even when you say the name of Jesus.

Another ingredient for power is faith and not fear. Faith in the word of God gives you confidence and makes you to believe that when you mention the name of Jesus something will happen and nothing can stand against it.

Walking and working under God's appointed authority is another thing that the disciples practiced. A believer who wants to exercise power over unclean spirits must be under God's authority. You must recognise that you did not earn the authority by yourself, but rather that it is inherent from God and is a right that has been given to you. It is important to note that the devil does not submit to you, or to us, as believers or as individuals because of our name, or because of our birth. He submits because of the power that we have as believers. If we pray, issuing commands in our own name, say, in the name of so and so, demons will not listen to us. But immediately we say, "In the name of Jesus," they will obey.

What happens during the new birth, i.e. when we give our lives to Christ, is that we are promoted from the rank of a Private in the army to that of a General. In the hierarchy of power, God has greater power than all the powers of darkness. Therefore the devil is always subject unto us, in Jesus name.

OVERTHROWING THE ENEMY'S KINGDOM

Another of our duties as believers is to overthrow the enemy's kingdom.

One of the ways we can do this is by contributing positively to the building up of the kingdom of God.

Dr. D.K Olukoya

We should acknowledge the fact that every single action that we take each day has an impact on, not only our own lives, but the lives of every other person that we come in contact with. We must, therefore, constantly examine ourselves to see how well our attitudes, behaviour and thoughts contribute to the building up of the kingdom of God. We must always be ready to set good Christian examples and tell non-believers about the saving power of Jesus Christ.

Our names must be known in hell as well as in heaven. The reason why our names must be known in hell is so that whenever we are praying, the beings in hell will say, "That is a believer, do not touch him!" But if you are living a careless life, you will not be able to operate with fire. Remember, the devil does not want your name written in the Book of life.

Everything you do must be geared towards pulling down the kingdom of darkness. Some people contribute towards the building of the kingdom of darkness consciously or unconsciously. If you commit sin, you are re-establishing the kingdom of the devil. When you are not walking in full obedience to God, you are contributing to the building of the kingdom of darkness. I pray that the Lord will help us to work on His side, in Jesus' name, Amen.

Before we attack the kingdom of darkness with some prayer points, let us make sure that the kingdom of darkness does not have a legal hold on our lives. I want you to pray like this:

"All the legal holds that unclean spirits have over my life, I command you to receive the fire of God now and be consumed, in the name of Jesus."

Your body must be under the control of your soul. Your soul must be under the control of your spirit. Your spirit must be under the control of God. If your spirit is not under control and in that line of authority, you cannot exercise authority over any other power. That is why you should talk to yourself like this: "My body, be under the control of my soul, my soul be in subjection to my spirit, and my spirit be in subjection to the Spirit of God, in Jesus' name.

PRAYER POINTS

1. I bind you devil, and all unclean spirits in every area of my life. I declare my life a danger zone for you, in the name of Jesus.

2. Anything that unclean spirits have eaten in my life, or whatever they have destroyed, be completely restored, in the name of Jesus.

3. I remove my name from the book of demonic casualties, in Jesus name.

4. I break every family covenant that may be affecting me negatively, in the name of Jesus.

5. I remove myself from the hold of any demonic power, in the name of Jesus.

6. I bind every spirit of infirmity, in the name of Jesus.

7. I break and loose myself from every bewitchment, in the name of Jesus.

8. Every link connecting me to evil things, break now, in the name of Jesus.

9. I reject any evil thing that I have inherited from my father and mother, in the name of Jesus.

10. I release all my helpers that are locked up in prison, in Jesus' name.

11. I invite the fire of God to destroy every evil altar constructed against my life in my village, town, or where I was born, in the name of Jesus.

12. I break every witchcraft curse, in the name of Jesus.

13. I bind every spirit of marriage destruction, in the name of Jesus.

14. I bind every spirit of untimely death, in the name of Jesus.

15. I bind every spirit of marital failure, in the name of Jesus.

16. I break every covenant of late marriage, in the name of Jesus.

17. I break every spirit of financial failure, in the name of Jesus.

18. I release my materials in satanic banks right now, in the name of Jesus.

19. I release myself from the hold of every evil remote controll ing power, in Jesus name.

20. I refuse to be controlled by any power, which is not the Spirit of God, in the name of Jesus.

21. I destroy the remote-controll ing powers, in the name of Jesus.

22. Any strongman attached to any bad thing happening to me at present, I bind you and paralyse you, in the name of Jesus.

23. Any evil that has been done to my l ife within the hours of midnight and 3 a.m. I cancel you, in the name of Jesus.

24. Any organ in my body that a strange hand has been laid upon, I set you free, in the name of Jesus.

25. Thank God for answered prayers, in Jesus' name.

CHAPTER TWO

Power
Against the
Spirit of
JEZEBEL

A lot of people are struggling and tiring themselves out with a closed door to which they do not have a key. In the absence of the key, banging, shouting, crying or generally struggling in an effort to get in, is a useless exercise. Unfortunately, this is the position of many Christians.

Jesus said unto Peter, "I give to you the key of the Kingdom and whatever you bind on earth, shall be bound in heaven and whatever you loose on earth, shall be loosed in heaven." Peter had a key. Paul too, had a key. Declare this loud and clear, "By fire, I receive the key that would open the door to my breakthrough physically and spiritually, in the name of Jesus."

The Lord intended our bodies to be His temple. But before the glory of God can fill a particular temple, it has to be cleansed and purged. Therefore, Jesus had to purge the temple at Jerusalem. He said to the Jews, "My house shall be called a house of prayer but you have turned it to a den of robbers" and He chased them out.

THE TEMPLE

As mentioned previously, the body of man is meant to be the temple of the Lord. But for many people, their body is not the temple of God but an entity which has virtually been caged or imprisoned by powers greater than them. I want you to proclaim liberty and freedom to yourself. The Bible says, "If the Son makes you free, you are free indeed." It also says, "where the Spirit of the Lord is, there is liberty" and also, "that Jesus came to proclaim liberty to the captives."

Pray: "Freedom of the Lord Jesus, soak me from the top of my head to the soles of my feet, in Jesus' name."

The Bible says, "If God be for us, who can be against us." When God is for somebody, anyone who decides to go against that person must be mad. If a witch, or wizard, or powers of darkness decide to wage war against a child of God, it would be the beginning of their end. In fact, it is madness to attack a child of the most High God.

A lot of Christians never grow because they spend 90 percent of their prayer time battling internal and external enemies and spend only 10 percent on their spiritual growth. When the spirit of freedom is upon you, anyone who turns against you is planning to run mad. Beloved, enough of useless battles. In many places in the Bible, God set the enemies of Israel, who had prepared and trained their armies to fight against the Israelites, against themselves. They destroyed themselves and made a way for the Israelites to move in and collect the spoil. This is why you must pray this prayer point: "Let all the enemies of my soul wage war against themselves, in Jesus name.

WHO IS JEZEBEL?

The first introduction to Jezebel in the Bible portrays her as the rebellious and domineering wife of a king called Ahab. She dominated and manipulated her husband. Unfortunately, for the nation of Israel, her husband happened to be their king.

"And Ahab, the son of Omri, did evil in the sight of the Lord above all that were before him. And it came to pass, as if it had been a light thing for him to walk in the sins of Jeroboam the son of Nebat, that he took to wife Jezebel, the daughter of Ethbaal king of the Zidonians, and went and served Baal, and worshipped him." I **Kings 16: 30-31.**

God had warned the children of Israel never to marry the Zidonians because they were idol worshippers. The same warning exists today that no believer should marry an unbeliever. If you do that in spite of the fact that you know that it is wrong, you have only constructed a coffin for your home. Eventually, it will become a foundational problem that will be very difficult to solve. This was what the king of Israel did. In addition to ignoring God's warning, he went on to further disobey God's commandment by serving the idol of Jezebel called Baal.

My prayer for bachelors is that they will never marry Jezebels, and the spinsters too will never marry Ahabs, in Jesus' name.

Ahab raised an altar for Baal and built a house for it in Samaria. The Bible says that Ahab did more to provoke the Lord God of Israel to anger than all the kings of Israel that were before him. The most important thing that we should all note from Ahab's story however, is that his problem started when he married Jezebel.

In the book of Revelation, Jezebel resurfaces:

> *"Notwithstanding, I have a few things against thee, because thou allow that woman Jezebel, which calleth herself a prophetess, to teach and to seduce my servants to commit fornication, and to eat things sacrificed unto idols. And I gave her space to repent of her fornication; and she repented not."*
> **Revelation 2: 20- 21.**

Jezebel, the wife of Ahab, was so powerful that she forced 10 million Jews to bow to Baal. Out of the entire population of Jews, only about seven thousand plus Elijah were faithful to God. In fact, Elijah thought he was the only one, until God said, "No, I have seven thousand more somewhere."

THE SPIRIT OF JEZEBEL

The woman Jezebel is now dead physically, but her spirit is still in existence and continues to cause many problems for Christians. This spirit has thousands of people in its grip. It is responsible for the worldliness and unseriousness you find in the lives and attitudes of so many Christians nowadays. It is the spirit converting many houses of God to entertainment halls, where people just go to be entertained by actors. It is the spirit of Jezebel that has produced a lot of psychedelic and disco Pastors.

These include Pastors with 'jerry curls' and 'Tyson' hairstyles. In such churches, you cannot differentiate between the Pastor's wife and a club girl. The spirit of Jezebel is responsible for the conversion of the house of God to a place of merchandise and a fashion show. This spirit of Jezebel is also introducing witchcraft into the house of God very cleverly and people are not aware of it. The spirit of Jezebel is responsible for the perversion of the authority in the

home, where the wife is converted to the husband
and the husband is converted to the wife.

Jezebel incited her husband to do evil which eventually
led him into trouble with the Almighty God. God
got fed up with Ahab and called a meeting of His
angels and said, "Which of you will go down and
deceive Ahab to die." They all gathered and gave
different suggestions. All that time, Ahab was
comfortable. Eventually, God put a lying spirit in the
mouths of Ahab's prophets; about four hundred of
them. All Ahab's prophets prophesied, "Go and
the Lord will give these people unto your hand." Only
one man was different, a true prophet of God. He
told Ahab, "No, if you go, you will not come back."
But that was not what Ahab wanted to hear.
Sometimes when a person is heading for destruction,
he or she would be deaf to every wise counsel. Instead
of taking heed of the warning, Ahab promptly
commanded that the prophet should be locked up.

THE EVIL QUEEN

The spirit of Jezebel is responsible for the revengeful
spirit in many believers now. A lot of believers want

to retaliate for what other people did to them just like Jezebel had wanted to retaliate against Elijah. This is wrong, because the Bible tells us that vengance is the Lord's.

The spirit of Jezebel is also responsible for the idolatry that is in the church now.

A man came to the house of God and said he was broke and that he wanted to be prayed for so that he would begin to prosper. Some brethren prayed for him. Shortly after, he went to his bank account, which had been dormant for a long time and found that somebody had mistakenly paid ₦30,000.00 into it. He jumped up and said that the Lord had prospered him. He went ahead and withdrew the money and gave testimony that God had prospered him. Beloved, that is modern idolatry.

The spirit of independence and ambition to be popular is another function of the spirit of Jezebel. It is the spirit that kills God's prophets prematurely. It is the power behind seducing spirits. The work of the spirit of Jezebel is so common nowadays.

All the 'panel-beating and spraying of the body' by Christians and careless eating are the works of the spirit of Jezebel.

THE NAME, JEZEBEL

What does the name Jezebel mean? It means 'without co-habitation.' That is, Jezebel will not dwell with anyone, unless she can control and dominate that person. It has destroyed preachers and politicians. It makes people to commit abortion, and is also responsible for many unsettled homes in our society today.

PRISONERS OF JEZEBEL

There are many secret prisoners of Jezebel today. These prisoners have no control over their sexual desire. They run after their house maids at night or any other woman, apart from their wives. Anytime they are not praying or singing praises to God, pictures of immorality fill their hearts. When you come across a man who enjoys being in the company of girls alone, know that he has a problem. If you know of a woman too, who prefers to be with men all the time, something is wrong somewhere. All these are secret prisoners of the spirit of Jezebel.

The truth is that the spirit of Jezebel would stop attacking a person only when it knows that the individual can withstand it. This is because Jezebel's worst enemies are the prophets of God who speak against it as the true prophet of God spoke against it in the Bible. The spirit of Jezebel hates repentance, prayer, holiness, purity and has captured many modern-day Christians. Some people go to church to seek deliverance, only for them to get possessed by the spirit of Jezebel. This then worsens their case.

THE FOUR POWERFUL STRONGMEN IN THE BOOK OF REVELATION

1. **The spirit of death and hell:** The first strongman is the spirit of death and hell. Death is the reaper while hell is the storehouse. So, one goes to work, and the other stores what is brought back.

2. **The spirit of the anti-Christ:** This is the spirit responsible for lukewarmness. It takes people farther away from the Lord knowing that the further one drifts away from the Lord, the deeper into darkness he or she will go.

3. **The spirit of Babylon:** This is the spirit of compromise. Believers should not compromise their faith at all.

4. **The spirit of Jezebel:** This message is centered on this strongman.

THE AGE LONG WAR

There has been an age-long war going on between the spirit of Elijah and the spirit of Jezebel. Elijah represents the interest of heaven, the call to repentance and a return to God. Jezebel, on the other hand, represents principalities or powers whose purpose is to hinder the work of repentance. Looking deeply into the Scriptures, we can see that Elijah was very bold. But Jezebel was also very bold. Elijah was violent against evil while Jezebel was violent against righteousness.

Elijah spoke about the ways of God while Jezebel spoke about the ways of witchcraft. They were at war in the Old Testament, and that war still continues today.

In the book of I Kings, we read about how Jezebel systematically murdered God's servants, i.e. the ones she could lay her hands upon. She wanted to eliminate Elijah too, but the God of Elijah kept him out of her hands. Ahab looked everywhere for Elijah and when eventually Obadiah found him, he said, "We have searched for you everywhere. You just locked up the windows of heaven and put the key inside your pocket. The king is looking for you."

But something happened in I Kings 18. There was a contest between the prophets of Jezebel and Elijah. The contest was on mount Carmel. The contest was very simple. The prophets of Baal, who were 450 in number, were on one side while Elijah was on the other side. Elijah said unto the people, "I, even I only, remain a prophet of the Lord; but Baal's prophets are·four hundred and fifty men. Call ye on the name of your gods, and I will call on the name of the Lord; and the God that answereth by fire, let him be God. And all the people answered and said, it is well spoken." So they began to call on the name of Baal and nothing happened. They did this for almost twelve hours.

The Bible says, "And it came to pass at the time of the offering of the evening sacrifice, that Elijah the prophet, came near and said, Lord God of Abraham, Isaac and of Israel, let it be known this day that thou art God in Israel, and that I am thy servant, and that I have done all these things at thy word. Hear me, O Lord, hear me, that this people may know that thou art the Lord God, and that thou hast turned their heart back again. Then the fire of the Lord fell and consumed the burnt sacrifice, and the wood, and the stones, and the dust and licked up the water that was in the trench. And when all the people saw it, they fell on their faces; and they said, "The Lord, he is the God; the Lord, He is the God." And Elijah said unto them, "take the prophets of Baal; let no one of them escape. And they took them and Elijah brought them down to the brook Kishon, and slew them there." And so will you slay your Baal today, in Jesus' name.

The God of Elijah is the God of fire. He will fight for you today against any spirit of Jezebel, in the name of Jesus. Now, after this kind of super victory, why on earth should Elijah run away and say that he wanted to die?

"But he himself went a day's journey into the wilderness, and came and sat down under a juniper tree; and he requested for himself that he might die, and said, it is enough now, O Lord, take away my life; for I am not better than my fathers." I **Kings 19: 4.**

This was Elijah talking because in verse 2, Jezebel threatened him. *"Then Jezebel sent a messenger unto Elijah saying, So let the gods do unto me and more also if I make not thy life as the life of one of them by tomorrow about this time."*

FEAR AND DISCOURAGEMENT

What came over the person who prayed and fire fell? How could such a mighty prophet turn and run? The answer is simple: Jezebel had released a flood of witchcraft and demonic powers against him.

It was not that the witches were eating up his flesh or drinking his blood. No, they could not. But they put two things in his heart to overwhelm him. These two things have also gained entry to the hearts of many people today. - fear and discouragement.

When fear and discouragement, as a result of an attack by the spirit of Jezebel, entered into the spirit of Elijah, the great prophet of fire turned and ran! This great prophet, who could easily have stood at the palace of Ahab and called down fire to destroy Jezebel and her whole household, turned and ran because two of the greatest weapons of the enemy were used against him.

A lot of people think that witchcraft is only about eating their flesh, drinking their blood and breaking their legs. No.

When there is fear and discouragement in a person's spirit, the person would run, even if it is only a cockroach that is talking. And then in that position of fear, the person becomes an easy target for the enemy. The enemy would be able to touch the person because he has not placed sufficient fire around himself. Witchcraft would first of all send its two disciples, fear and discouragement. If you allow them to touch you, then they start opening the way for others to follow. They discourage people so much that they would not be able to pray well and then they start thinking it is 'one man somewhere' attacking them. These two powerful weapons are what the spirit of Jezebel uses commonly today.

Elijah went away in the chariot of fire. John the Baptist came in the spirit and power of Elijah. And the dancing daughter of Herodias got John killed. She danced very well and Herod the king promised to give her whatever she wanted. The girl now said, "I want the head of John the Baptist." So, the man who came with the spirit and power of Elijah was killed just like that. What the spirit of Jezebel did to Elijah, Herodias also did to John the Baptist. Before John was beheaded, the two evil disciples of Jezebel had attacked him; that is, fear and discouragement.

The attack was so bad that John sent a messenger to Jesus asking, "Are you the one that is to come or should we look for another?" Here was the forerunner of Jesus Christ who said, "Behold the Lamb of God, who taketh away the sins of the world." He baptised Jesus, yet he sent a messenger to Him to find out who He was, because fear and discouragement had entered into him

THE SPIRIT OF ELIJAH

The ministry of Elijah is not over. In fact, the book of Malachi tells us that towards the end of time, God will send Elijah to us again.

> *"Behold, I will send you Elijah the prophet before the coming of the great and dreadful day of the Lord. And he shall turn the heart of the fathers to the children, and the heart of the children to their fathers lest I come and smite the earth with a curse."*
> **Malachi 4: 5-6.**

God is still raising up a company of prophet Elijahs. These are spirit-filled Christians who are supposed to kill the prophets of Jezebel and drink the blood of the prophets of Baal.

But you cannot be in the company of Elijah if Jezebel still has a hold on you. One fact you should note about your enemy is that if it cannot attack you directly, it will seek to bring you into sin, thereby positioning you for the judgment of God.

The movement of the power of the spirit of Elijah is what we need now to put the spirit of Jezebel to flight. Addiction, adultery, arrogance, broken marriages, fear, fornication, jealousy, unclean thoughts, masturbation, perverted sexual relationships, spiritual blindness, the spirit of religion, witchcraft and all occult involvement manifest in the lives of those who are controlled by the spirit of Jezebel.

For example, if the spirit of Esau were upon somebody, the person would sell his birthright, meaning that the person would stay at the tail instead of at the head. If the spirit of Manasseh were upon somebody, the person would also operate at the tail region. If the spirit of Pisgah were upon somebody, the person would be seeing good things but would never taste them. If the spirit of Saul were upon somebody, the person would start off on fire for God and end up with the spirit of witchcraft. If the spirit of Pharaoh or Herod were upon somebody, good things would die at infancy in their lives.

THE ANOINTING KILLER

The spirit of Jezebel is the spirit that kills God's anointing in people's lives. Such people would receive no revelation. They pray and see nothing, and/or hear nothing. This spirit kills the prophet inside you. It is the spirit that pushes people under God's judgment as in the case of Ahab. Jezebel kept pushing Ahab until he got into trouble. The spirit of Jezebel is the spirit that prefers artificial glory to the glory of God. It is the spirit that causes constant strife in the home. It turns husbands into babies and wives into giants. It is the spirit of immoral activities.

"And when Jehu was come to Jezreel, Jezebel heard of it; and she painted her face, and tired her head, and looked out at a window. And as Jehu entered in at the gate, she said, Had Zimri peace, who slew his master? And he lifted up his face to the window, and said, Who is on my side? Who? And there looked out to him two or three eunuchs. And he said, Throw her down. So they threw her down: and some of her blood was sprinkled on the wall, and on the horses; and he trod her under foot." **2 Kings 9: 30 −33.**

Beloved, today, you have to throw the spirit of Jezebel out of your life. Let the dogs lick her blood and you will trample upon it. Jehu had no mercy for Jezebel. He was not ready to reform Jezebel. There should be no mercy or compromise or sympathy towards the spirit of Jezebel. Jehu trampled her under foot, and we should do the same. Right now, God is giving you the spirit to participate in the internal judgment of Jezebel. You have to cast her down. Let the judgment of God come forth. It is time for the children of God to unite against this spirit with the power of the Holy Spirit, under the Elijah anointing and the anger of Jehu. Start to proclaim holy war against the spirit of Jezebel.

WAY OUT

There are six ways to deal with the spirit of Jezebel operating in the home. The devil tries to keep people from understanding these facts.

1. **Do not raise your voice against your spouse because the Bible says that a soft answer turneth away wrath.**

2. **Identify the issue.**

3. **Do not dig up old wounds.** Bringing up old wounds will further increase the tension.

4. **Do not call your spouse names.** This is character assassination.

5. **Do not generalise by telling your spouse, "You** always do this or do that." All these are destructive exaggerations.

6. **Finish the discussion.** Do not burst into tears or get out of the house in anger.

PRAYER POINTS

Please, pray the following prayer points with holy anger.

1. You spirit of Jezebel, I command you to release your captives, in Jesus' name.

2. You spirit of Jezebel, you shall not kill the prophet of God inside me, in Jesus' name.

3. I cast down every evil imagination against me, in the name of Jesus.

4. I break any ungodly association with the spirit world, in the name of Jesus.

5. O Lord, set my enemies in array against each other, in the name of Jesus.

6. Lord, give me the key to open the way unto my breakthrough physically and spiritually, in the name of Jesus.

7. I pull down the altar of witchcraft against my life, in the name of Jesus.

CHAPTER THREE

POWER *Through* FIRE BAPTISM

You must read this chapter carefully and prayerfully, especially if you are not satisfied with the present state of your spiritual life and truly desire an improvement.

"Now Moses kept the flock of Jethro, his father in law, the priest of Midian: and he led the flock to the backside of the desert, and came to the mountain of God, even to Horeb. And the angel of the Lord appeared unto him in a flame of fire out of the midst of a bush: and he looked, and, behold, the bush burned with fire, and the bush was not consumed. And Moses said, I will now turn aside, and see this sight, why the bush is not burnt. And when the Lord saw that he turned aside to see, God called unto him out of the midst of the bush and said, Moses, Moses. And he said, "Here am I. And he said, Draw not nigh hither; put off thy shoes from off thy feet, for the place where on thou standest is holy ground. Moreover he said, I am the God of thy father, the God of Abraham, the God of Isaac, and the God of Jacob. And Moses hid his face; for he was afraid to look upon God." Exodus 3: 1-6.

We find one of the most important events in Scripture in the foregoing. The Bible has been divided into what Bible students call dispensations, which means different periods of time. This particular time signaled the beginning of what we call the 'dispensation of the law'. It tells us about one man called Moses.

People have said a lot of things about the bush that refused to be consumed. In the desert, you find a lot of dry leaves, dry trees, cobwebs, bird nests and all kinds of things that are inflammable. These things were in that bush while the fire was on, yet it was not consumed. They were good materials for fire yet the fire did not use the bush and its contents as its source of fuel supply.

THE ENERGY OF FIRE

The fuel that supplied the energy of the fire was not from that bush, the fire sustained itself. So, it was not an ordinary fire. The focus of the fire was on Moses. Moses saw it, turned aside and there he received his call. And the Bible tells us that of all the prophets, there was none like Moses. He was the only one who spoke to God face to face.

He was a very important man of God. If you read his history you will find that even the devil tried to kill him at a young age just as the devil tried to kill Jesus at a young age.

Sometimes, when we say, "Pray against the spirit of Herod," many people don't understand what we mean. The spirit of Herod is the spirit that kills good things in infancy. Herod was the man who killed all the babies below two years because he wanted to kill Jesus. The devil tried to kill Moses by the side of the water where they put him but God prevented that. The devil tries to kill many people because he knows what God would do with their lives.

Moses went to the best university in the world because Egypt was the best centre of learning in the world at that time. He was also learned in all the wisdom of the Egyptians because he grew up in the palace of the king.

THE WILDERNESS

The incident we are describing now happened at Mount Horeb. Horeb means a waste or a wilderness.

All men of God must pass through the wilderness. Moses passed through his own wilderness. Elijah, John the Baptist, and even Jesus our Lord passed through their own wilderness. Jesus was there for forty days and forty nights. All holy men of God and anybody at all who wants to be useful to God must get to that place in his life, the place where fire is burning the bush and the bush is not consumed.

Moses died at the age of 120 years. He spent his first 40 years in Egypt. It ended in disaster because he ended up as a murderer. Why? Because he tried to use his own power, the arm of flesh which we know will always fail to deliver God's people. After this he ran away from Egypt at the age of 40 to a place called Midian where he worked as a shepherd; a job hated by the Egyptians. He did not know that during that stage God was teaching him the principle of shepherding, for a time was coming when he would lead three million people in the wilderness. It was like Peter who was first taught how to catch fish so that he would know how to catch men.

THE BURNING BUSH

Moses saw the burning bush when he was eighty years old. That was the moment he met God and his life never remained the same again. His life became meaningful and now had a purpose. He knew why he was called. He discovered the purpose of God for his life. There are many people who do not know God's purpose for their lives and as a result they are doing the wrong thing. In summary, Moses spent the first forty years of his life thinking that he was somebody. He then spent the second forty years learning that he was nobody. And then he spent the last forty years seeing what God could do with Mr. Nobody. He did not know what to do until he came across the fire.

> *"All darkness shall be hid in his secret places: a fire not blown shall consume him; it shall go ill with him that is left in his tabernacle."* **Job 20:26.**

Job discovered the fire that nobody prepared with fuel. It is men who have moved like this that can be useful to God in any form.

"John answered, saying unto them all, I indeed baptize you with water but one mightier than I cometh, the latchet of whose shoes I am not worthy to unloose, he shall baptize you with the Holy Ghost and with fire. Whose fan is in his hand, and he will thoroughly purge his floor, and will gather the wheat into his garner, but the chaff he will burn with fire unquenchable."
Luke 3:16-17.

John the Baptist was a powerful messenger. The Bible tells us that he wore a leather belt and clothes woven from camel's hair; the Bible also tells us that his food was locust and honey. Jesus told us that amongst those born of women, none was greater than John the Baptist. He was the forerunner of our Lord Jesus Christ.

THE QUALIFIED

A study of the life of John the Baptist reveals that he had a lot of wonderful qualities and one unforgettable one was that he was very precise in everything he did. He said, "I baptise but my own baptism is with water, somebody else is coming who shall baptize you with the Holy Ghost and with fire." A lot of people know about water baptism. We thank God for it because when we are baptised in water it is the symbol that we have died with Christ and resurrected with Him. It is good. Also when you are baptized in the Holy Spirit you may speak in tongues, you may prophesy and all kinds of things may happen.

But very few people know what we mean by baptism of fire. In fact, many who claim to know what it means do not really know. But verse 17 makes it very clear. Chaff is the refuse of grain and the straw of the corn. In those days, in the land of Israel, when people wanted to remove the chaff from the corn, they would tread upon the corn until the chaff was removed. Then they would separate the chaff from the grain and burn it with fire because if they did not do that, the wind would have blown it back into the grain which they had cleaned.

THE WHEAT

The wheat represents the good in our lives, that which is produced by the Holy Spirit. The chaff represents the evil in us, produced by the flesh.

The Lord knows how to separate the wheat from the chaff. Sometimes, when He does it to us, we feel the heat in a particular area of our lives which we love dearly and are not ready to let go of. We all have some items in the showroom of our lives that are not valuable to God. Sometimes when God begins to touch these things, we complain that the pain is too much, whereas it is the refining heat of God.

When God passes you through fire, you will come out a better vessel to serve the water of life to people. God will use both cold and hot vessels. If you are in the house of God now and you are hot for the Lord, He will use you and if you are cold, He will use you. You may wonder how God may use you if you are cold. If you are cold, God will use you as an example for others not to follow. He did this to the children of Israel many times. When they did the wrong thing, He disciplined them so that nobody would follow them. But if you are hot He will use you to minister grace to others and as an example for others to follow. The only kind of people God will not use at all are the lukewarm people. He will just abandon them on the shelf. They would be a stock on the shelf like expired materials. So you should allow the fire of God to do a deep work within you today.

THE DARK DAYS

A long time ago, this country was thrown into heavy darkness. Human sacrifice was common and a lot of horrible things happened. Anyone who wore good clothes did not wake up the next morning. People were afraid to call witches by name, they called them nicknames because they were afraid that they would die.

In some places in Nigeria, witches actually went about in daytime, people ground day old babies in mortars to use for medicine, some people received up to 2,000 incisions and we had many evil trees growing in different arears. Sometimes when men of God attempted to cut down these trees, blood would start coming out from them, or sometimes by the following morning, the trees would start growing again as if they had not been cut the day before . People's lives were regulated by superstition. You could not whistle at night or call a snake by its name. Some hunters shot at animals which turned into human beings. Many rocks and stones demanded worship and if they were not worshipped, there was trouble.

We were told about a king who had a magical cutlass which used to spark fire. As a reult of this, people were afraid of him. But then something happened. God raised up certain men in this country who received more than the baptism of the Holy Spirit and the gifts of speaking in tongues and body vibrations. They received the baptism of fire. These men entered forbidden forests, stopped the killing of twins, silenced powerful demons and chased them out of their hiding places. One of these men got to this king and commanded the cutlass to be powerless and its sparkling ceased immediately.

FIRE BAPTISM

The blunt truth is that there are many people with the baptism of the Holy Spirit but there are very few who have received the baptism of fire. Those who have received the baptism of fire do not mind whether another person is annoying them or not. There are certain characteristics that you will notice in them. Virtually anywhere in the Old Testament that God appeared, fire was always present. Fire symbolises the presence of God, i.e. the Unquenchable Fire. We remember the God of Elijah, the God that answered by fire.

A piece of iron would not bend easily unless you put it into fire and it becomes hot. The reason some people have not been bent, and still have crooked places in their life is because there is no fire in them. Therefore, God says, "Okay, I abandon you to your situation." God will not abandon me to my situation, in Jesus' name.

When you go through the baptism of fire, God will reschedule your life. A lot of people are scheduling their own lives after their parents who made mistakes and are now in hell fire. They say, "Because my daddy was a member of this place I must be there and die there." May God have mercy on them. God is crying, "Be rescheduled, be rescheduled," but they refuse to be rescheduled.

People hate change so much that they fail to realise that change is what brings progress. It is because they have not passed through the baptism of fire and so God finds it difficult to bend them. He just abandons them. The lame would be beating the drum while the leper would be singing and a child of God who has not been rescheduled would be dancing.

This is very unfortunate, but the truth is that a lot of people around now are just like that. Until you listen to that rescheduling cry of God, many unclean things won't find their way out of your life. This is one of the blunt truths in the word of God. Raw gold just dug out of the earth never looks good. But when it is passed through the fire to remove the impurities, it comes out clean.

The reason unclean spirits and all kinds of evil things are still hiding in some people's lives is that there is no fire in them. Beloved, we need the fire of God in our midst and when it comes in, the promises contained in the word of God shall come to pass. The strangers would fade away and run out of their hiding places, because when the fire comes in, it does not spare the ants, the elephant or the snake; it burns everything. The sad part is that many people are afraid of what will happen if they dare get on fire. If you are like that, you need to be rescheduled because this may be your final call.

The absence of the baptism of fire is the reason some people are so slow when it comes to spiritual development and the things of God. All they do is speak in tongues: "Baba bakakaka," and immediately after that, they sleep and the night caterers come and say, "Well, you have blown your tongue, it is time for night meal." And the person who was speaking in tongues now begins to consume food, which weakens his spiritual life.

How can unbelievers be running after you, a Christian girl? You are praying for a Christian husband and it is only married men and unbelievers who find you beautiful. Something is wrong somewhere. Something has to be burnt in your life to remove that magnet inviting evil people to you.

FIRE COOKS

The lack of fire is also the reason why many people start the race wonderfully but lose their way down the line. Fire symbolises power and lack of it means powerlessness. Fire produces light and without it there would be darkness.

Have you received the baptism of fire? Lack of this baptism is why many Christians are suffering. A Christian who is not interested in progress has no fire. A Christian who is not excited about the things of God has no fire. A Christian who gets weighed down by long prayers has no fire. If certain things are still coming upon you to press you down on your bed while you sleep, it is because there is no fire in you.

Witches and wizards roam around the house freely when they know that the occupant is spiritually cold. Some people are in a hurry to escape from God's presence. When they are in the house of God, they are always in a hurry to leave and engage in other activities. To some, prayer and fasting is very difficult, and this is because there is no fire in their lives. Some people come to the Mountain of Fire and Miracles Ministry and say, "I thank God that my prayer life has changed." However, we are not only asking for your prayer life to improve, but for it to get on fire, and cause tragedies in the kingdom of darkness when you open your mouth to pray!

Perhaps your Holy Ghost baptism is just speaking in tongues. You forget that there is a difference between you possessing the Holy Spirit and the Holy Spirit possessing you. The Holy Sprit will not possess you until you have passed through the baptism of fire, because when the chaff is still there, it means that fire has not burnt it. With chaff still present in your life, the Holy Spirit cannot possess you fully. It can only enter and operate in a little way. But for total possession, fire has to fall.

You want to reign with Christ always, but never once in your life have you seen a vision of heaven. What you see are masquerades, night caterers, and serpents. With which Jesus do you want to reign when these are what you are seeing? When others say, "I saw angels of the living God praising God in heaven, and I joined them; it was so wonderful." But you on the other hand are saying, "I saw snakes." You should be ashamed of preaching the gospel under such situations.

Many are just conquerors but not more than conquerors. Somebody who is more than a conqueror will not only conquer, he will also take captives. How many captives have you made for the Lord? You are still busy sewing tight skirts so that everybody can see your figure. I ask again, how many captives have you won for the Lord? Many people are praying that they want to grow but it is not coming from their hearts. Something within them is saying, "No, you cannot grow."

It is lack of the baptism of fire that makes it difficult for people to run away from strange things and situations. All the virtues of many men have been buried under the sea by strange powers that have collected their sperm and have stored it there. This is all because there is no fire in their lives.

When you receive the baptism of fire three things will happen:

1. There would be no spiritual lethargy

"Then I said I will not make mention nor speak any more in his name. But his word was in mine heart as a burning fire shut up in my bones, and I was weary with forbearing, and I could not stay." **Jeremiah 20: 9.**

When you receive the baptism of fire you cannot relax. It is not possible because the fire will not let you. You cannot see sinners and feel unconcerned. You would not be able to do without prayer and you would find it difficult to be away from your Bible. You would want to sit down and read it through. That is what we call baptism of fire.

2. You will preach with fire in your bones

"For though I preach the gospel I have nothing to glory of: for necessity is laid upon me, yea, woe is unto me, if I preach not the gospel." **1 Corinthians 9: 16.**

You will be unable to stop preaching the gospel of Jesus Christ. You will become such a threat to the kingdom of darkness that the occult, or witchcraft practitioners will mark you out and avoid you.

3. **There will be a spiritual overflow.**

"Behold, my belly is as wine which hath no vent; it is ready to burst like new bottles. I will speak, that I may be refreshed I will open my lips and answer." **Job 32: 19-20.**

The power of God would be burning within you. You will wake up in the night speaking in tongues. God will be talking to you and you will see what God wants you to do. You will not live in darkness or semi-darkness.

Have you received the baptism of fire? A pregnant woman who had the baptism of fire went to the market and mistakenly stepped on items an idol worshipper had displayed for sale. The idol worshipper jumped up and started raining curses on her while she was apologising. The idol worshipper then cracked his sticks and fire began to come out of his mouth.

This pregnant woman said, "I quench that fire in your mouth, in the name of Jesus," and the fire was quenched. The man said, "What did you just do?" She replied; "I spoke to your fire, in Jesus' name and secondly, I returned all your curses to you, in Jesus' name." When the man heard that, he ran away. If the woman had no baptism of fire, it would have been a terrible day for her. In fact, the power of darkness could have changed her baby from there.

Unfortunately, a lot of people are becoming friends with fire extinguishers. What quenches the fire of God?

FIRE EXTINGUISHERS

1. **Lust:** When your imagination indulges in uncleanness.

2. **Idolatry:** If you permit anything to come between you and your God, it becomes an idol. For example, your job, money, etc.

3. **Laziness:** Life of ease at home, lack of zeal for the things of God and hatred for long prayer sessions.

4. **Over-sensitivity:** Bitterness rises quickly in the hearts of some people immediately somebody disagrees with them.

5. **Judgmental spirit.**

6. **Gossip:** All gossips are the devil's advertisers.

7. **Worry:** This is when you are anxious about the future.

8. **Selfishness:** This is when you ignore the interest of others and are interested only in yourself.

9. **Distraction:** This is when you are unable to focus on Christ and you find it difficult to read the Bible and gain something from it.

10. **Lying.**

11. **Discouragement:** Some people are easily discouraged. At the first sign of failure, they run away. They quit when things are hard.

12. **An abusive tongue:** Some people cannot control their temper, or the words which come out of their mouth when they are angry.

13. **Depression:** This is when you allow despair to overwhelm you. You think of your problems and withdraw from everybody. But the Bible says, "I will not despair for I have believed to see the goodness of the Lord in the land of the living."

14. **Fear:** All kinds of fear are fire quenchers.

15. **Procrastination:** This is when you are always planning to go higher and dig deeper but always postponing the day you will start.

16. **Lack of sexual control:** People in this category should forget about spiritual growth.

very hard to ensure that people will not receive the baptism of fire. When the baptism of fire falls on a person, he can prophesy for up to five hours non-The enemies of our soul have the most powerful scanning machine that you can think of. They can look and locate our weaknesses quickly. They work stop. Many unclean things will be drawn out of his life. He or she would not have to pray to be delivered, because the fire will answer everything. All infirmities would disappear. When fire falls on fibroid or whatever it may be, it would melt away because God did not create you with it. It is chaff and fire has to burn it.

Beloved, if you are ready today, I want you to bow down your head and begin to ask the Lord to forgive you for any sin that would prevent the fire from falling upon you, because during the prayer session the fire will fall and things will burn and you will be catapulted to a higher realm. You will go from the position of weakness to that of power.

When some people came against Elijah and extended the invitation of failure to him, he said, "Instead of me to come down, let fire come down." And that was how 102 people were roasted. The third group of 51 people that came to him adopted a different approach because they were afraid to die.

When you are in Elijah's position, which enemy is it that can sit on your brain or your business? There would be no need for you to go to the hospital when you have the Great Physician.

Please, if you are not ready for the fire that would come down as you pray, don't pray.

PRAYER POINTS

1. Holy Ghost fire, fall upon me now, in the name of Jesus.

2. All strangers, loose your hold, in the name of Jesus.

3. O Lord, crucify me on your altar now, in the name of Jesus.

4. O Lord, set me on fire by the Holy Ghost, in the name of Jesus.

5. Everything that is cooperating with evil in my life, cease to cooperate now, in the name of Jesus.

6. My life, begin to cooperate with the Holy Ghost, in the name of Jesus.

7. All the negative things that I have been eating, I refuse to eat you any more, in Jesus' name.

8. Fire from God, fall upon my life now, in the name of Jesus.

9. *(Stretch forth you hands as you say this:)* Lord, put the head of my Goliath in my hands, in the name of Jesus.

10. My enemies shall bow down before me, in the name of Jesus.

11. O God, make me a vessel of your power, in the name of Jesus.

OTHER BOOKS BY DR. D. K. OLUKOYA

1. 20 Marching Orders To Fulfill Your Destiny
2. 30 Things The Anointing Can Do For You
3. 30 Prophetic Arrows From Heaven
4. A-Z of Complete Deliverance
5. Abraham's Children in Bondage
6. Basic Prayer Patterns
7. Be Prepared
8. Bewitchment must die
9. Biblical Principles of Dream Interpretation
10. Born Great, But Tied Down
11. Breaking Bad Habits
12. Breakthrough Prayers For Business Professionals
13. Bringing Down The Power of God
14. Brokenness
15. Can God Trust You?
16. Can God?
17. Command The Morning
18. Connecting to The God of Breakthroughs
19. Consecration Commitment & Loyalty
20. Contending For The Kingdom
21. Criminals In The House Of God
22. Dancers At The Gate of Death
23. Dealing With The Evil Powers Of Your Father's House
24. Dealing With Tropical Demons
25. Dealing With Local Satanic Technology
26. Dealing With Witchcraft Barbers
27. Dealing With Unprofitable Roots
28. Dealing With Hidden Curses
29. Dealing With Destiny Vultures
30. Dealing With Satanic Exchange

Dr. D.K Olukoya

70. Let Fire Fall
71. Limiting God
72. Lord, Behold Their Threatening
73. Madness Of The Heart
74. Making Your Way Through The Traffic Jam of Life
75. Meat For Champions
76. Medicine For Winners
77. My Burden For The Church
78. Open Heavens Through Holy Disturbance
79. Overpowering Witchcraft
80. Paralysing The Riders And The Horse
81. Personal Spiritual Check-Up
82. Possessing The Tongue of Fire
83. Power To Recover Your Birthright
84. Power Against Coffin Spirits
85. Power Against Unclean Spirits
86. Power Against The Mystery of Wickedness
87. Power Against Destiny Quenchers
88. Power Against Dream Criminals
89. Power Against Local Wickedness
90. Power Against Marine Spirits
91. Power Against Spiritual Terrorists
92. Power To Recover Your Lost Glory
93. Power To Disgrace The Oppressors
94. Power Must Change Hands
95. Power To Shut Satanic Doors
96. Power Against The Mystery of Wickedness
97. Power of Brokenness
98. Pray Your Way To Breakthroughs
99. Prayer To Make You Fulfill Your Divine Destiny
100. Prayer Strategies For Spinsters And Bachelors
101. Prayer Warfare Against 70 Mad Spirits
102. Prayer Is The Battle
103. Prayer To Kill Enchantment
104. Prayer Rain
105. Prayers To Destroy Diseases And Infirmities
106. Prayers For Open Heavens
107. Prayers To Move From Minimum To Maximum
108. Praying Against Foundational Poverty
109. Praying Against The Spirit Of The Valley
110. Praying In The Storm

Dr. D.K Olukoya

Dr. D.K Olukoya

YORUBA PUBLICATIONS
1. ADURA AGBAYORI
2. ADURA TI NSI OKE NIDI
3. OJO ADURA

Dr. D.K Olukoya

FRENCH PUBLICATIONS
1. PLUIE DE PRIÈRE
2. ESPIRIT DE VAGABONDAGE
3. EN FINIR AVEC LES FORCES MALÉFIQUES DE LA MAISON DE TON PÈRE
4. QUE l'ENVOUTEMENT PÉRISSE
5. FRAPPEZ l'ADVERSAIRE ET IL FUIRA
6. COMMENT RECEVIOR LA DÉLIVRANCE DU MARI ET DE LA FEMME DE NUIT
7. COMMENT SE DÉLIVRER SOI-MÊME
8. POUVOIR CONTRE LES TERRORITES SPIRITUELS
9. PRIÈRE DE PERCÉES POUR LES HOMMES D'AFFAIRES
10. PRIER JUSQU'À REMPORTER LA VICTOIRE
11. PRIÈRES VIOLENTES POUR HUMILIER LES PROBLÈMES OPINIÂTRES
12. PRIÈRE POUR DÉTRUIRE LES MALADIES ET LES INFIRMITÉS
13. LE COMBAT SPIRITUEL ET LE FOYER
14. BILAN SPIRITUEL PERSONNEL
15. VICTOIRES SUR LES RÊVES SATANIQUES
16. PRIÈRES DE COMBAT CONTRE 70 ESPRITS DÉCHAINÉS
17. LA DÉVIATION SATANIQUE DE LA RACE NOIRE
18. TON COMBAT ET TA STRATÉGIE
19. VOTRE FONDEMENT ET VOTRE DESTIN
20. RÉVOQUER LES DÉCRETS MALÉFIQUES
21. CANTIQUE DES CONTIQUES
22. LE MAUVAIS CRI DES IDOLES
23. QUAND LES CHOSES DEVIENNENT DIFFICILES
24. LES STRATÉGIES DE PRIÈRES POUR LES CÉLIBATAIRES
25. SE LIBÉRER DES ALLIANCES MALÉFIQUES
26. DEMANTELER LA SORCELLERIE
27. LA DÉLIVERANCE: LE FLACON DE MÉDICAMENT DE DIEU
28. LA DÉLIVERANCE DE LA TÊTE
29. COMMANDER LE MATIN
30. NÉ GRAND MAIS LIÉ
31. POUVOIR CONTRE LES DÉMONS TROPICAUX
32. LE PROGRAMME DE TRANFERT DES RICHESSE
33. LES ETUDIANTS A l'ECOLE DE LA PEUR
34. L'ETOILE DANS VOTRE CIEL
35. LES SAISONS DE LA VIE
36. FEMME TU ES LIBEREE

ANNUAL 70 DAYS PRAYER AND FASTING PUBLICATIONS
1. Prayers That Bring Miracles
2. Let God Answer By Fire
3. Prayers To Mount With Wings As Eagles
4. Prayers That Bring Explosive Increase
5. Prayers For Open Heavens
6. Prayers To Make You Fulfil Your Divine Destiny
7. Prayers That Make God To Answer And Fight By Fire
8. Prayers That Bring Unchallengeable Victory And Breakthrough Rainfall Bombardments
9. Prayers That Bring Dominion Prosperity And Uncommon Success
10. Prayers That Bring Power And Overflowing Progress
11. Prayers That Bring Laughter And Enlargement Breakthroughs
12. Prayers That Bring Uncommon Favour And Breakthroughs
13. Prayers That Bring Unprecedented Greatness & Unmatchable Increase
14. Prayers That Bring Awesome Testimonies And Turn Around Breakthroughs